These Mothers of Gods

Rachel Bower

First published 16th July 2021 by Fly on the Wall Press
Second print run 15th December 2021
Published in the UK by Fly on the Wall Press
56 High Lea Rd, New Mills, Derbyshire, SK22 3DP

www.flyonthewallpress.co.uk
Copyright Rachel Bower © 2021
ISBN: 9781913211554 Paperback
978-1-913211-58-5 EBook

For my Mum

Praise for 'These Mothers of Gods':

"In Rachel Bower's powerful new collection, you will find mothers displaced, mothers deceived, mothers labouring to stay sane and alive. But woven amongst any vulnerability is a fierce celebration of the mother-body, opened up to prove the unique and complex stories each one holds. I am grateful to Bower for finding these women - historical, biblical, autobiographical – and offering me such inventive, arresting poems, brim-full with blistering truths."

- Rebecca Goss, Poet

"Powerful, compelling and exquisitely crafted, These Mothers of Gods is a tour-de-force of female-focussed storytelling."

- Teika Marija Smits, Writer and Editor

"Rachel Bower's poems show us mothering as we've never seen it before, through time, history, and mythology. The collection centres the voice of the other, while conveying poignant experiences of joy, elation, triumph and hardness. These image-rich verses are poems of intense curiosity and beauty."

- Jason Allen-Paisant, Author of *Thinking with Trees*

Acknowledgments

Grateful acknowledgments are made to the following publications, in which some of these poems first appeared: *Anthropocene*, *The Banghor Literary Review*, *Frontier*, *The Interpreter's House*, *The London Magazine*, *Magma*, *The Mechanics Institute Review*, *New Welsh Reader*, *Stand* and *Wild Court Magazine*. I am also grateful to the editors of the following anthologies: *Islands are Not Mountains* (Platypus Press); *The Result is What You See Today* (Smith | Doorstep), in which two of the poems were first published.

I owe a debt of gratitude to Isabelle Kenyon at Fly on the Wall Press for believing in this book and for her tireless work on behalf of writers and books that will change the world. My deep thanks also go to members of the University of Leeds poetry group and to the online 3030 group, for their encouragement, wisdom and friendship. I am profoundly grateful to the following poets for their inspiration and guidance in editing some of these pieces: Jason Allen-Paisant, Charlotte Ansell, Malika Booker, Carole Bromley, Kimberly Campanello, Vahni Capildeo, Suzannah Evans, Mick Gidley, Rebecca Goss, Shaun Levin, Helen Mort and John Whale.

As always, I owe heartfelt thanks to my family and many friends, too many to name, for their unceasing support and encouragement. To my Mum, to my Dad, to Dewi, to Marilyn and Jonathan, to Julian and Poppy. And to my sister, Sarah, for being brave and brilliant – the best.

Finally, I thank Jake for his belief, love and support over all these years, and to my amazing kids, Jude, Esme and Otto, who continue to inspire me with their open hearts and fierce sense of justice. There would be no book without them.

Contents

Water Birth

Mediterranean Sea

Nobody wants to be born at sea
but I'm a midwife: *squeeze my hand,*
that's it, we've got this girl.
She squats, *not time to push,*
bile rising with the swell. *Breathe*
through the surge, keep your head.

The baby's well positioned, head
down, curled and smooth like a sea-
sucked pebble. *That's it, keep breathing,*
squeeze those ice-packs in your hand,
cool the bruises down. I push
hair from her eyes, scrap of girl,

clothes soaked in petrol. The girls
had been shoved in a dinghy, heads
barely covered, then pushed
off from the shore in a sea-
coffin. We hauled her up, women's hands
helped from behind. We hold our breath

now for the baby. I say, *keep breathing*
but English means nothing to this girl,
we need Arabic for *breathe* and *girl* and *hand*.
The translator's sick as a dog, headed
up for fresh air on deck. The sea
swells, nearly time to push

but now she's trying not to push,
juddering through breaths
of thick fog, sick pea soup and the sea-
fire is swallowing it all, burning this girl
up so she blazes. When the head
crowns she grips, scorches my hand.

I make a cave of her face with my hands,
and tell her, *yes it is time to push,*
it is time, I can see the head,
so push now, nearly there, breathe
through closed lips and yes girl,
push against this wave, against this sea

that would swallow us all, head out, final push
and in my hands, a breathing girl
a beautiful girl, a salt pearl birthed at sea.

Immaculate

Do you know, she swallowed an emerald,
touched a peacock. It was one of the seven
stars. Stainless. An angel in a terrible
dream came to her, told her of lemon

bolts of lightning, of arrows to the womb.
He was found inside a peach, floating on
the sea. In a glowing stalk of bamboo.
Emerged from her forehead, prodigal son,

fully formed. He burst from rock as a flash.
She stepped into a giant footprint, tucked
a ball of feathers in her belt, it was the gash
of a falling moon. The Great Bear looked

into her eyes. It was the stork against a blood
sky, swinging a bundle above the flood.

Flood

Jamalpur District, Bangladesh

A mother stands at the front
of a raft, looking straight

ahead. She bends from the waist,
presses down with a bamboo stick.

The water reflects marigolds
from her green silk sari.

Her feet are bare, tired.
She does not think of grilled corn

or sugar and rice pounded to lai.
Lime trees wait on the horizon

casually kicking brown water.
This is not a lake so there is no shore.

Toxic Blooms

330 Savanna Elephants, 400 Pilot Whales

the whales tiny \ in the aerial footage
silver black mackerels \ shore litter

the elephants \ sleeping toys
trunks greyish \ ready \ for play

bluegreen waterholes \ stunning maps

but on the ground
biologists retched \ wept \

at the bulk \ the curves \ the unbearable weight
rotting \ luxuriant \

the shining \ beaching \ bleaching
hulks

herds \ pods \ families
all slacked into sand

Gypsophila Paniculata

Baby's Breath

It is impossible to see
starry white flowers

in this darkless ward
so I am blind

to the blossom
around his mouth.

The doctor observes
the blooms of his exhale,

he is breathing too fast
just look at his chest,

it shows in his blood.
I don't think so, I say,

but when the scent
stains his sheets

and the buds set
little hooks in my throat

I trample around the room
in search of tiny petals.

Cannula

After Matthew Siegel

A lifeguard
in sea green
presses gauze on her baby's hand,
tapes the pad. *He's okay,
it'll be over soon.*

She trickles sweet syrup
into the crying cave of mouth
as instructed.
Hold his arm firm now.

Her breasts leak,
a turquoise vein swells.

She once stood to her chest
as the tide crept in, foot planted
where she'd dropped the bright ring.

A needle
in a haystack.

She wrestles the tiny arm,
fails to protect it.

Saline slips
down the tube, stinging cold.

All done. He was good as gold!

She gathers him up,
clumsy splint arm,
and wades for dry land,
his hurt salt in her blood.

Stepmother

and I'm caught like a fish in a box on the wall in this pebble-dash castle
by the sea, a donkey-driver's wife, never meant to be, like this, and yes, I
promised I'd make her mine, but that bone-white skin of theirs I'll never
share, father to daughter, generations trudging it out on the salt flats, back
and forth with that pack of mules that would trample my breast given half
the chance, and I never asked for flags or trumpets but maybe a glance of
thanks, for wiping and sweeping, defending her with my life

and I feed her fresh liver and lungs at breakfast when he's out, for strength,
for blood red lips – thread her bracelets of shells, for protection – the
neighbours always watching, twitching if we step out the gate, ready to
report – *they went down the market, the bakers, the sands*

and always her cold hand small in mine. Just this morning, a man slipped
her an apple on the pier – I snatched it in time, pared out the poison with
my trinket knife – an anniversary gift whittled sharp on the rocks. I passed
her only the sweetest flesh, chewed first in my mouth to be sure

and he's started to say he doesn't know me – *you're not the woman I married*
*– eyeing me with suspicion from their sofa – *you was a stunner back then – a*
beauty – his lips round his beer, money-belt hanging fat in his crotch. He
wants us both, timeless, behind glass

and it's the same every night, every day in this cul-de-sac on the cliff. I
pocket the change in the market, drag her round the arcades, combing
slot-machines for coppers. I am building our reserves, letting the mirror
rust under the mattress, under his sleeping bulk, money-belt even tighter
round his waist, stinking of dung – biding my time, plotting our way out of
donkey town

Wet Nurse

Halimah bint Abi Dhuayb, Wet Nurse to Muhammed

He was never mine to lose, unless you count
the milk fat thighs, creased at the knees,
the eyes, drenched clean with manna sap
from my own breast, teeth, sharp as kittens

his cry of '*um halmah* in the night, *halmah*
until dawn, and all was right as rain except
this was the desert and his real Ummi's breasts
were rock as she handed him over, my gift

to wipe streaks of yellow curd on boulders,
tuck hamaat figs in his cheeks, drape blue glass
beads at his neck, surrounded by prints in the sand
from a thousand foxes, tented ears alert

to the loss of this milkchild, the eager arms
of the mother, the pain of handing him back.

Birth Mother

Aminah bint Wahb, Mother of Muhammed

At the feast to mark his return, a lamb crowns our table but
My old sickness comes back – I can stomach only flatbread, dry fatir
In my mouth, clutching at my tongue. My gut clenches with the
Nausea of those early weeks, bound to a sunlight seed, and the
Animals talking again, dogs snarling hush woman – patience –
He will come. My bones quarried to sculpt his spine, my

Breath gave flight to his heart. I retch now, throat scorched, curl
Into the seashell of my body. Hollow. He'll be three now, might
Not know me – will he like fried onion, cardamom, cloves?
The broth broils yellow moons in his honour. Light does not shine

Within my face this time, but streams down my belly, thighs,
Ankles instead – bright tributaries crackling my body,
Hips stretchmarked maps of powdered gold. I try to cover the shine
But when I finally lift him to my face, his cheeks glitter with ore.

Light

Sicily

I was searching   for that pause   at the end   of the out-breath
   when I saw the woman   from the tent   next door

sitting   on a camp-chair   at dawn   drawing deeply
   on a cigarette   Inhaling   the last

of the night   feet on cool sand   a moment   of rest
   Four kids   still slept   in dark nests

                  unaware
   of this dawn-woman   in their mother

I was careful   not   to catch   her eye
   looked   silently up   at linen skies

We both knew   all around
   sprites were stretching   in lilies

butterflies unrolling   new wings   water-
folk   spooling   indigo wool   unravelling   pale silk

I observed   all this   our ghosts
   of lime-flower air   and cotton tread

before the birth   of the day
   and the gentle   return   of the in-breath

Little Marys

After Blaubart (Bluebeard), 1977, choreographed by Pina Bausch.

There is no climbing to be done in here —
this is a place of citrus and snow

of caressing the walls with purple lips
for the taste of parchment in plaster —

the scent of the waxy skin
of the women who came before us. They crackle there

still, under magnolia, charging our nylon dresses
and ballet toes as we hang, suspended like puppets

without wires. Our strings were cut,
or sometimes removed, before we came here

and now there is no way to move us
or make us speak or tap our feet —

we are ghost shrimps, icefish and jelly frogs.
Not translucent dolls without organs

but dreadful women with nothing left to lose.

Madwoman

After William Empson

You don't want madhouse in your bed, in your room,
near the children, shouting at strangers in the street –
that big red building with the clock will soon
sort it out – you don't want madhouse under your feet,

in the kitchen, warbling with the birds, you don't want it
spoiling the soup, wandering the pavement in slippers,
beating the hedge with a stick, stashing eggs in hair thick
with wild. Madhouse is a liability, send it off, the jitters

are unnerving. Madhouse is devious, needs a shock,
morning exercise, doctors with mouthgags to put
it right – to work wonders, oil the feathers, lock
it all away. You don't want madhouse, send it off. But

no – keep it in the family – imagine the shame,
getting the funny farm involved. You should bolt it in,
keep madhouse close to your chest, protect your name
from helpful neighbours, don't wash that dirty linen –

even if madhouse tries to lift your wings,
keep it down, keep it in – do not let madhouse sing.

Mother/ Not Normal

"The location of the 796 infants and children who died in the [St Mary's Mother and Baby] Home between 1926 and 1961 is unknown." (Kimberly Campanello, MOTHERBABYHOME)*

permanently restless   *refuses food*

even whip clean   air   like   white egg

and porridge   clear with   holy

water   *resists interference*   bones fragile

as porcelain   *weeps*   *at times*

without cause   pear   drops

sherbet   lemons   sugar   mice

in her mind   *delusional*

imagines   wrongs   at the   hands

of the sisters   speaks   yellow

eyed   of wolf pups   born *blind*

deaf   still   head   hanging

low   walks   softly   claws

at her breasts   unwanted   shrines

of   pale   packed   ice

* Italicised words are direct quotes from Campanello's *MOTHERBABY-HOME*, a work which is composed entirely of text taken from historical archives and other sources related to the Home.

Haibun Meltdown

Svalbard archipelago, Norway

Picture the game where you rip a piece of newspaper in half every time the music stops. The children crowd unnaturally close on tiny pieces of print. Soon they will start to fall off. I catch one, collect his tears, but do not know where to tip them. I decide to freeze them in little blocks for later. The party is ruined, children flapping everywhere.

dazzling blue ice-caps
cracked to polystyrene bits
floating in blackness

Silver Seal

After Louise Glück

There is a time to kill, to slick after fish,
to dive. A time to gorge, to get,
to blubber, to fill.

A time to pup, to spill,
to rend.

There is a clumsy time,
sanded,
greyish barrels spotting dunes

a milk time, to fast, to thin,
teeth like dogs,
a shadow time, guarded,
feather foot
suckling time.

A time to leave
little snowy casks
stranded,
flippers to sky,

a time for bulls
and cows
to roll
lush-bellied, viscous
and heavy, a wanting time.

A time to return,
plunge, heal,
a time to swell again.

Newborn

Wrecked on the seabed, she births a creature of the deep. Pebble unfurling, starfish hands circling. Conductor of waves, doctors, tests. The mouth opens, small O, closes again. She hulks in soft mud, untethered, unsafe.

Harvest red algae,
simmer to pulp, roll with oats:
feast on laverbread.

Between sludge and light she blunders with the giant head, hers now, slipping. Weedy neck. Bright mouths grin under rocks: lemon-eyed welcome parties. She kicks off, tangled, attempting a rise.

Pluck forests of kelp,
soak with milk, nutmeg, ginger:
gulp salty mouthfuls.

She is underwater jerking limbs, exhausted, clinging to her gift. Hard pink gums, mossy fists beating slow. She stares at glittering trails. Cockles cleave to her shins. He is turtle-heavy, trusting, as she flails: clawing towards the promise of sun.

Flags and Flowers

There is no document of civilization which is not at the same time a document of barbarism. (Walter Benjamin, Illuminations, trans. Harry Zorn)

the carpet   at the Test Centre   was pencil blue   blue of lead

water   blue with unforgiving   grey weave of blue suite   the wind blew sweet

of our belongings   cruel sweet   too dead for snowdrop blue   and the screen

flashed electric   blue glasses   on the man opposite   blew his sweat chill

shivering   as the timer flew   on our chances   of belonging

bucketing crosses   of salt on sky   blood on snow   my pencil all wrong

for this test   indecisive fingertaps   cold numb   clicking rose   thistle

forget me not   while Flashy Eyes   jabbed Cenotaph   confident

Roast Beef   definitely   the Queen   blue blood   Fawkes blew it

up   Shakespeare   haunting the flame   between green and violet   the V

of dark bellied geese   never at home   blown away

with trying to belong   red dragon   snap dragon   white blue flame

forgotten   my practice   bog cotton   or Whitehall   my son

knows it all   from school   Black Death   Union   blue willow

plates but my brain   mists mountain   speckled eggs   cyan

steel   clear   the meter   out of credit   cold bean tongue

tinned blue lace   under thin skin   at our wrists   and throats

birds   crawling at our feet   carpeting   our toes

Story of Baking, Story of Birds

After Gboyega Odubanjo

the pie was plum – he sat in the corner and put in his thumb and
said, you're only my babymum, so no, sweet one, I cannot marry
you, for I have a wife at home – no, stop, that's not quite right –
actually, it was bird – he kept me in an eggskin shell and said he
kept me very well with four and twenty blackbirds tender under
rusk and I longed for beak ruptured crust, for sockets pecked to
dust – but no, that's wrong – I said, pat me and prick me and
mark me with B, grind my bones to make your bread – not real-
ly, I wouldn't stand for that – I stepped upon a blackbird, alight,
rib cage spread of toes, flight – hooked the basket high in the oak
with that wise old owl, rock a bye baby on the tree top – but no,
he lobbed rocks, brought us both down, broke my crown, vine-
gar and brown paper, stamped on the blackbird, splaying wings,
breast, throat – no, don't worry, wrong song – hush little baby
don't say a word, papa's gonna buy you a mocking bird – but the
last pie was air, hollow as bird bones, wafer-thin – so I said, baby
we'll eat broth without bread, no diamond ring no looking glass
no whipped no sent to bed no plum no bird no bloody pie

Drought

Purulia District, West Bengal

The sky is a shriek, the earth a fractured bowl.
The potter throws dirt from her wheel,
thumbs caked with patali gur,
thickly baked to gloves.

Tiny pylons march on the horizon
like ants, carrying the spoils of heat
high above their heads. A wasp grub
crackles, but there will be no escape.

A baker's bicycle bumps over bedrock,
buckle of wheels,
no ghee to billow the dough, only dust.
The land thirsts for mishti doi.

Vixen

After W. S. Merwin

She nudges her cubs out, nose to head, as alert to threat
as they are ignorant, tumbling around her feet, pushing

her crouched legs straight. They jumble for milk, heat
between teeth as she looks ahead, scans the bush

for tremors, amber eyes bright. She is sturdy, little trace
of *light paws running*, streak of rust, clearing the fence –

slacker now, heavy with birth but the glowing face
betrays her – she will fly again, out like a flame if she senses

danger, slick into the night. But for now, she is maternal,
nosing them back underground. No trickery here, curling

a nest of dusty cubs, no perfect, hotly-packed but gentle
in this dark gathering of blood, bracken and hearts unfurling.

In a Manger

The cattle are lowing, yack the men of the inn,
knowing it's Mary, woman under each arm
bearing down next to the donkey, out in the barn.
The kettle boils brightly, the women bring gin-

soaked cloths to swab the trough, disinfect the floor
so it shines under bright skies, under her cries
of *don't leave me, I can't do it, don't let me die*
fire in the coccyx as Joe waits at the door

wondering should he come in and sweep
or go back for a drink, get his head down,
then someone grabs him, the head is crowning,
shoves him to Mary and he holds her, deep

in the earth as a star looks down where she lays
this belly-strong woman, birthing on hay.

Late Show

Midwives juggle babies, rainbow sleepsuits flashing
as Toddlers race past, urine pots balanced on their heads,
hotly pursued by Consultants on stilts, sequins sparkling,
Roll up, roll up! It's the Greatest Show on Earth!

The Calliope rings down in Special Care,
doors swinging, banging with the Big Top Band
that never stops. Nurses march to the crash of the glockenspiel
as Windjammers blast the brass. *Ladies and Gentlemen,*

Step Right Up! It's the International *All Star* Circus!
Fire-Breathers cook, Matron serves up on spinning plates
hoops whirling on her hips, as Milk Ducks waddle
around the ring, squirting fake flowers at the crowd.

I hold you tightly in the dark, breathing popcorn hair
as Angel Tattoo soars high above our heads, sprinkling
our faces with sawdust. For a split second she is falling
but the Ringmaster shouts, *The Show Must Go On!*

Christmas Day, Daughter Arriving

After Toi Derricotte

You arrive early, impatient and purple
but beautiful, gaping for milk, small fists

battering without aim. The turkey's on freeze
for New Year, won't be missed.

The midwife arrives just in time to sweep
you from the pool, after a sneaky turkey dinner

with her grown-up kids, swift half stout —
here to welcome you as one of the winners,

bursting into our world of tinsel
and trees, what a cracker you are

— our bubbles, our flaming plum pudding,
and since you're all we need, we pour

ourselves clumsily upstairs, bed very far
from the world, our brightest Christmas star.

After the Stork

Four Hours Postpartum

She brought her body to the shower room
as instructed. Bloated strawberries disperse
at her feet, inking the stream. The soft dome of stomach

comes too, stones stitched in the gut
of the dozing wolf. She pushes it aside to see the feet,
swollen and mauve, submerged to the ankle.

Rooted in this murky puddle,
bruised and emptied, she is more alone
than ever before. The sting of hot water

comes as a relief, rinsing a deluge of sobs
and offal, pouring brightly on leaking breasts.
There is no mirror to steam, no need to see the face.

One day, she will turn the silver dial to the right,
strap a thick white pad between her thighs,
and shuffle to the ward, hungry to claim him back.

Slump

Batagaika Crater, Northern Yakutia, Eastern Siberia

I

A single larch
totters on the rim

of scooped earth,
roots jutting

through dust
in full sun.

Needles fall
with the thaw

sprinkling
an ancient foal.

A bison calf
slips unsteadily

into mammoths
and elks.

II

Day-trippers hike
the kilometre

to the crater
for picnics

and black tea
on the edge

but locals stay away
from this gateway

to the underworld
with rightful dread —

the modern-day
bottomless pit.

Even devils
freed from

the permafrost,
clinging

by their nails
to crumbling walls

crusted in sweat,
shriek

help help
as tourists

scuff hot sand
in their eyes

then sprint back
to the bus

to the rasp
of a falling tree.

Woman in the Grain Bin

Çatalhöyük, Anatolia

I wish I could love you, Seated Woman,
stretched breasts
dissolving time, streaming milk into your lap
over stout calves to red earth, swinging

slightly, for the clamp of hard gums,
belly slacked
over that seam that spills
babies to mud. You sit

fronting me, shoulders proud,
sacred, squeezed
from clay while I look away,
dry, close my knees, bra politely padded.

Shedding

10 weeks old

As he grows
stronger, rounder, smoother,
she begins to rattle inside her skin,
paper-thin
across the stomach,
a crinkled blouse
draped over dough.

The breasts, still milk-full,
in time will shrink, crease,
then the eyes will cloud,
the skin crack
near the mouth
and she will peel it right back

and   slither   out
bright   new   clean.

Then she will reel in shock.
That cast skin was the tale
of their becoming.
Panicking, she'll hunt down
the scraps,
gather strips

scrunch them tightly at the waist
and twist
to the flare
of bronze chiffon,
sashay their story
through the town.

Hive Mother

'Or will I be a different mother, whose body has not been a room, whose breasts contain no nourishment?' (Gail McConell, *Fothermather*)

It all needed doing that summer – the work that gets seen, on show in golden comb, row on row of gleaming white brood – curled perfect c – perfect sees – tightly-packed pollen, powdered yellow – and the rest as well – cleaning and scouring the darkest nooks, chewing up food for the littlest – nurses evicting waste – faeces, muck, the dead – twirling them high above our heads, shifting, mending, cooling

with dislocated wings – we're all builders, mothers, guards in this place and it's not about who sees it – everything still needed doing – that summer the drones wandered in, square bodied and obscene, sucking their fill – leaving dirt and disease – and I forced out the thinnest flake of wax to fill a crack, all our field bees out

hunting for salts, for resin to seal the gaps – flying their wings ragged, thoraxes bald, crawling back to our dark to dance – not for the fun of it, almost on their knees – but because we needed it, at the heart of the hive, waggling heat, angles, hope – the exact coordinates of a poppy.

Matryoshka

Sheffield, UK

I'm crackling over black ice towards her — in her
usual place — crouched by the bridge over the beck
where rats run colossal — there's no way round,
not now — you have to pass her bleaching shrink-
ing every time — crimson scarf, bluebell eyes, can-
dy cheeks — all robbed by the light, and this morn-
ing she's whispering snow flurries and I'll have to
sneak past but I fumble — turn back with feeble
coins that force her hands to pray thanks at the
tiny wooden bundle at her heart — the last secret
lashings of scarlet and gold.

Run for your life

run your body free of small hands
so your body is there to give when you get home,

run without bags, dusk cracking yolk in your hair,
past people walking ghost dogs, pissing gold on trees,

run your body free, past the tawny screeching to her love,

kwikk to his call, *kwikk* to his call,

run your body free, past the tawny screeching to her love,

past people walking ghost dogs, pissing gold on trees,
run without bags, dusk cracking yolk in your hair,

so your body is there to give when you get home,
run your body free of small hands,

run for your life.

All the Pretty Little Horses*

From The Black Book, edited by Toni Morrison

'I am a black woman holding a white child in her
arms singing to her own baby lying unattended in the grass'
– Toni Morrison, 1973

                                          Hushaby, don't you cry

'Sir John Hawkins, a slaver licensed by Queen Elizabeth, transported his
human cargo in ships named *Jesus, Angel* and *Grace of God*' (10)

                                          Go to sleepy, little baby.

'People said he freed her because she was his own daughter; she was
_____ daughter. I know that I have seen him come out of her mother's
room many a morning' (1862)

                                  When you wake, you shall have cake

'Slaves took food to runaways; would accept beatings rather than reveal
hiding places' (18)

                                  And all the pretty little horses

'and they sold us like beasts, and they counted our teeth. . . and they tested
the lustre or dullness of our skin' (Aimé Cesaire)

                                Blacks and bays, dapples and grays,
                                  Coach and six-a little horses.

'Brown University at Providence, Rhode Island, was established in 1764
from the fortune made by the Brown brothers whose wealth was based on
the profits made from their ships in the African slave trade' (10)

'She said, "I'm going to kill you. These black titties sucked you, and then
you come out here to beat me." And when she left him, he wasn't able to
walk' (18)

'My mother had about three masters before she got free... There wasn't no use for no one man to try to do nothing with her. No overseer ever downed her' (19)

There's a poor little lambie

'my master purchased me knowing I was stolen from my mother and father'
(Pennsylvania Packet and Daily Advertiser, 20 May, 1788)

The bees and the butterflies pickin' out his eyes

'She has four children, one a girl of about 13 years of age, another 7, a boy about 5, and an infant 11 months old. 2 of the children will be sold with the mother, the others separately, if it best suits the purchaser' (Public Sale of Negroes by Richard Clagett)

The poor little thing cries, "Mammy"

'My mammy name Phoebe. Pappy have to git a pass to come to see Mammy, before the war' (19)

'I inquired if she was not excited almost to madness when she committed the act. No, she replied, I was as cool as I am now; and would much rather kill them at once, and thus end their sufferings, than have them taken back to slavery, and be murdered by piecemeal' (A Visit to the Slave Mother Who Killed Her Child, 1856)

Hushaby, don't you cry

'In Central City she [Clara Brown] operated a laundry and tried to acquire enough money to purchase freedom for her husband and children.' (51)

Dress made by slave, origin unknown – Remnant of bedspread made on a plantation – Coverlet, handwoven by a slave – Bedspread woven by slaves – Hand tufted slave-made piecework quilt – Eight-pointed star – Silk from a dress worn at a ball – Bedspread – Handwoven rug – Bedspread – Piece-work quilt – Dolls made for white children by a slave named Emmeline

'I am not complete here; there is much more'
– Morrison, 1973

Go to sleepy, little baby

* This lyric essay is made up entirely of quotations from *The Black Book*, edited by Toni Morrison (Middleton A. Harris, 1974). Page numbers are referenced in parentheses. *The Black Book* states that '"All the Pretty Little Horses" is an authentic slave lullaby; it reveals the bitter feelings of Negro mothers who had to watch over their white charges while neglecting their own children.' (65).

TV Haibun

She looks suspiciously at my breasts through the screen. My own sack baby
nestles on my chest; brimful of pearl. These breasts leak more milk than he
could ever drink. The girl infant is still staring: it would be dangerous to
meet the eyes. Dusty ribs, she is dry. Her mother's body, flat: gave every-
thing to grow this child: nothing more to give. My folds ripple the story
of his birth; provide fruit. It is too lush. She looks away, light as butterfly
bones. I hoped for babbling but she is arid. It scorches there, while we eat
snow. I glance at glowing logs, shift, careful not to wake him, plump and
content. I wish my petals were not closed to her. *Come, gorge here. You are
mine too. Ours. Come, drink, I am yours*

melting butter sun
drip light on dust, yolk on sand
syrup on dry land

Hive Mother II

Vivace. On repeat.

| |:   *librarian - cleaner - donor*
         sister - doctor - neighbour

         cousin - flatmate - best-mate
         school-nurse - nanna - midwife

         teacher - mentor - auntie
         baker - colleague - carer   :| |

Mother 'In Law'

Ruth and Naomi

Naomi said *leave me* —
no more sons in my womb
to   marry   now

go   home   Ruth
you are young
enough

but I stayed with this mother
made mine
in promise   not in blood

where you go   I will go
where you stay   I will stay

gleaned the scalp   of earth
as she instructed
dust   cracked   hands

stubble barley   burn of throat
dipped my bread   in vinegar
let the new man   eat

drink to merry heart sleep
uncovered   his feet
in the threshing shed

curled   until dawn
a   secret
between us all

and so it was done —
her man came good
bought us   with the fields

we were homed wheated
bellyful   the baby
made mothers

of us both
the neighbours saw him
at her breast

Naomi's line
restored   by me
daughter in kind   not in kin

Becoming

After Maggie Nelson

Every child is a god
to the *many gendered mothers*
of its *heart*   trickled syrup

by a host of nurse
bees   swollen sweet
capped   with wax

and the keeper who watches
her bee   unpick
its cell

to emerge   lake-eyed
fur-peached   honeycomb
caul torn

yearning for bee bread
knows
the rightful

expansion of moth…er
is   moth   flicker
That the hummingbird

hawk moth
whipping up lilac
in a blur of wings

is tiny fat bird
and insect
both

drawingnectar
up the skinny proboscis
beak

that there are moth-ers
who set night-traps to catch
slivers of fragrant wood

but by dawn the trap is still empty
bereft after cold
spring winds —

they have   flown
to join the host
of mothers

the hostia
of heraldic bees
sailing

through laurel smoke
and every child is laurus nobilis
evergreen

to the many gendered   moth...rs
of its heart
tirelessly

injecting tarn breath
into hexagon   after   hexagon
of gods

and   look   !   here it comes now
that shivering new bee
ablaze   with care

Hive Mother's Prayer

May the nights bring you pollen
and sun-bright sheets, may the hours

we rocked you still lull you
to sleep, may they offer relief,

may all your nights open with bee-bread
and honey, release you from grief

may they hold tired feet, may your head
remember the warmth of my cheek,

may your nights close in a glimmer
of wings, may your belly keep its heat.

Faith

Bradford, UK

The Mother on the top deck
reading *Calm Parents, Happy Kids*

Section Two, How to Manage
Your Anger, cursed this morning

when he refused his shoes.
Her belly cramps with guilt

as she mutters a vow to do better.
She pats her leopard-print scarf,

rifling the pages for extra time, patience,
cash, a house in the country

with fields, sticks, dens,
headlines that are kind.

The boy's lunchbox still in her lap.

*

He's on the bus
without lunch, rattling

with worry. The teacher
offers facts about wood, steel,

plastic – he keeps his hand
down – doesn't say if you soften

your soles enough
water becomes slate underfoot

that bread multiplies with faith,
that bones settle to stone.

One boy splits a secret —
they head out to play

hang off each other's necks,
rush to the hall —

no-one wants to be last.
A girl spots his burning face,

blags him a plate of chips and beans,
marches him over to her mates.

*

The girl's on the bus
with the hard kids.

He keeps his head down
seat bristling his thighs, can't laugh

along with his stuck mouth.
They spit out of the window

when he gets off. His Mum
scrubs his hair hard, tries to knit

him a hat. It takes weeks
to loop the yarn

into hooks and purls,
a jumble of holes

but soft as a moth
in his pocket.

Wordling

A baby blackbird hops madly at the base of an oak
unable to get lift. It lurches from tree to tree,
unlucky.

A conker falls too soon. When the child stamps
she finds only a pale heart nestled in velvet,
embryonic.

Offal falls from the womb. Crocuses sprout under paving.
A chicken spots a streak of wet yolk and crumples,
aghast.

These are noises in the throat, not yet formed.

Fortune

the cellophane fish
curled on her palm
promises *luck*

but she's not sure

knows when oarfish rise
to shallow waters
quakes are near

a bad omen

spiny dogfish passed
off for cod, neatly
parcelled in paper

with a smile

tyrian purple, the smell
of clotted blood,
deception

or *indifference*

black plastic
invisible to the eye
of the optical sorter

even *plenitude*

five loaves and two fish
full of plastic, all
hoping for miracles

for lucky stars

Smog

Hebei Province, China

no blue sky this year
only a sour yellow taste
in the heart and throat

*

There is a photo. A woman and boy play ping-pong outdoors. The tap of
the ball is smothered. The noses and mouths are masked.

*

Hebei has China's worst air pollution. Shahe is one of its major sources of
pollution.

(*South China Morning Post*, September 2017)

*

Air Quality: Purple. Very unhealthy.
All groups may experience serious health effects.

*

Factories in Shahe, the 'City of Glass', produce about 160 million weight
cases of flat glass annually, 20 percent of all glass produced in China.

(*China Daily,* February 2017)

*

etched, aluminium, float, sheet, green, blue, gold, pink, grey, mirror,
marble, reflective, patterned, clear, tempered, louver, jalousie, silver,
turquoise, cobalt, terrazzo, garden, lacquered

*

Sand is the raw material in glass production. The factories are surrounded
by fields. The fields are lined with corn. The corn is coated in sand

*

The   Sandman   is   coming

*

Go on try it. Tip your head back. Drink sour air.

*

Smog, *n*. 2. *fig.* 'A state or condition of obscurity or confusion; something designed to confuse or obscure.'

(*Oxford English Dictionary*)

*

Oxford, UK.
Air Quality: Green. Good.
Ideal for outdoor activities.

*

Populations in low-income cities are the most impacted by polluted air.

(World Health Organisation Ambient Air Quality Database, 2018)

*

Little drops of water.
Little grains of sand.
Make the mighty ocean,
and the pleasant land.

('Little Things' Julia A. F. Carney, *Gospel Teacher*, 1845)

*

the furnace billows
thick white steam, clotting bright and
almost beautiful

Changelings

Devaki and Yashoda

*

She has your nose, Devaki lies to her husband,
he has your chin, Yashoda murmurs to hers.

Each drapes a string of pearls under the proud
belly of her gift-child, searching for her own scent
but finding only the other woman.

Devaki dotes on the girl, lavishes laddu, blossom, figs.
As she rubs plump thighs with sandalwood,
she knows their time will be short.

Yashoda worships the boy, scatters coral, lotus, dates.
She rocks through burn, until his legs fall heavy as pebbles.

*

Babies sleeping at last,
the women drop like stones,

oceans apart, wrecked on shores
with ransacked wombs, little limbs

their bodies did not grow.

Hungry mouths in oily deeps

sleep, new baby, sleep
– our only hope –

but small cries, earthly,
command them back.

*

breasts stinging
to serve the gift-child,
grey spray milk

for blistered lips,
preparing to learn
the creel of limbs

unfelt in the womb,
to coax songs
and stories from

a brooding girl,
eight arms budding,
destined for skies –

a twirling boy,
waves and mountains
bright in his yawn –

these foster mothers
of changelings, hopeful
mothers of gods.

Continue on Loop

We all fall down in the ring of roses.
Crushed rice cakes spill from my pocket.
Flushed, I wipe the parquet floor, keep singing,
down at the bottom of the deep blue sea,
catching fishes for our tea! A mug of milky
brew goes cold. *Atishoo, atishoo, we all jump*

up. I am sweating. *My baby is a jumping*
bean. I escape the church hall, inhale roses,
the baby on my back, crying for milk.
I kneel to steal a petal for my pocket
then regret it — he is louder now. I see
a dog, point it out hopefully, singing

the Mary had a little lamb song
as I rush to cross the street, jumping
at a car that I'd missed. I see
a mother pram pushing towards me, rosy
and serene, nothing flying from her pockets.
My breasts sting tightly, let down milk.

We just need to get home and you can have milk
I yell to the baby in my best sing-song
voice, *we'll be there soon.* I grope my pockets
for snacks and speckled frogs jumping
into pools. He arches, the wail rises,
shattering glass like the banshee. I can see

our street. Home. We are in. The neighbour sees
me pull out a breast, plug the scream with milk.
We sit, he glugs, I breathe. Swap sides, then I rise
to change him, lie him on his gym, sing
as I empty the bin, pull out wet washing, jump
a plastic king, a shepherd, a brick. I pocket

the chocolate for later. Tissue in a pocket
so the washing goes back in, *a sailor went to sea sea*
sea, feed the baby in his highchair, dab his jumper,
his chin, his shining cheeks. The milk
bottles clink when I put them out, and I sing
of green bottles, the invisible work of the rose

the falling of petals, the swell of sea, the rising
again from severed stems, and we jump up and sing
of pockets of rye, then lay close together in milk.

About the Author

Rachel Bower is an award-winning writer based in Sheffield. She is the author of *Moon Milk* (Valley Press) and *Epistolarity and World Literature* (Palgrave Macmillan). Her poetry has been published widely in journals and magazines, including *Magma, The London Magazine, Frontier, New Welsh Review* and *Stand*. Her work has been commissioned by a range of organisations including BBC Radio (National Poetry Day), Collections in Verse (Poet in the City/ The British Library), Barnsley Museums and Apples and Snakes North.

Rachel edited the *Verse Matters* anthology with Helen Mort (Valley Press) and is currently editing a parenting anthology with Simon Armitage (Faber & Faber). Her short fiction has also been widely published, and she won *The London Magazine* Short Story Prize 2019-20 and the W&A Short Story Competition 2020. She is currently teaching Creative Writing at the University of Leeds.

https://rachelbower.net/
Twitter: @rachelebower

Photo Credit:
Joe Horner

About Fly on the Wall Press

A publisher with a conscience.
Publishing high quality anthologies on pressing issues, chapbooks and poetry products, from exceptional poets around the globe.
Founded in 2018 by founding editor, Isabelle Kenyon.

Other publications:

Please Hear What I'm Not Saying
Persona Non Grata
Bad Mommy / Stay Mommy by Elisabeth Horan
The Woman With An Owl Tattoo by Anne Walsh Donnelly
the sea refuses no river by Bethany Rivers
White Light White Peak by Simon Corble
Second Life by Karl Tearney
The Dogs of Humanity by Colin Dardis
Small Press Publishing: The Dos and Don'ts by Isabelle Kenyon
Alcoholic Betty by Elisabeth Horan
Awakening by Sam Love
Grenade Genie by Tom McColl
House of Weeds by Amy Kean and Jack Wallington
No Home In This World by Kevin Crowe
The Goddess of Macau by Graeme Hall
The Prettyboys of Gangster Town by Martin Grey
The Sound of the Earth Singing to Herself by Ricky Ray
Inherent by Lucia Orellana Damacela
Medusa Retold by Sarah Wallis
Pigskin by David Hartley
We Are All Somebody
Aftereffects by Jiye Lee
Someone Is Missing Me by Tina Tamsho-Thomas
*Odd as F*ck* by Anne Walsh Donnelly
Muscle and Mouth by Louise Finnigan
Modern Medicine by Lucy Hurst